THE GOSPEL OF THE KINGDOM

Dallas Willard for a New Generation

Christian A. Dickinson

Title: *The Gospel of the Kingdom*
Subtitle: *Dallas Willard for a New Generation*
Written by: Christian A. Dickinson

Illustrations by: Learning Engineered LLC
Published by: Learning Engineered Publishing®
Library of Congress Control Number: 2026930998
ISBN (Print Paperback): 978-1-965741-58-0
First Edition: 2026
Printed & Created in: United States of America

Text and Illustration Copyright © 2026

Learning Engineered Publishing® (U.S. Reg. No. 8,057,038) is a division of Learning Engineered, LLC, and a subsidiary of Carpe Diem Unlimited Holdings, Inc.

LEARNING ENGINEERED
PUBLISHING®

CONTENTS

EPIGRAPH

"The message is not the message.
You are the message."
— T. Austin-Sparks

"Start children off on the way they should
go, and even when they are old they will
not turn from it."
— Proverbs 22:6 (NIV)

ACKNOWLEDGEMENTS

To my father, David V. Dickinson, whose early faith planted seeds that took years to sprout.

To Coach Neff and Coach Duggar, who taught me discipline, courage, and what leadership costs.

To Nick, whose God-timed friendship led me to Dallas Willard and the life with God I thought I'd lost.

To Josh, for showing me what it looks like to raise boys in the gospel of the kingdom—with strength, steadiness, and joy.

To my wife Morgan and five children who have watched me stumble, repent, grow, and want to be a better man: thank you.

And to God, for the grace that keeps writing straight with crooked lines.

DEDICATION

To my children and grandchildren,
I'm not writing this to impress strangers.
I'm writing it because I'm terrified you're going to live your whole lives as Christians and still miss the very thing Jesus came to give.

This is the best inheritance I have.

I love you more than you'll ever know.
— Dad / Granddad

And to my eighteen-year-old self, the week after Dad died.
I wish someone had handed me this then.

How This Book Finally Happened

I grew up in a living-room church.

No building. No budget. No pastor on payroll. Just a dozen families crowded onto couches and folding chairs while my dad and a few others opened the Bible, drank bad coffee, laughed easily, and talked about God like He was actually present.

And He was.

The kingdom of God didn't feel distant or abstract. It felt close. Normal. Alive. Following Jesus wasn't a program—it was a way of being human together. That was the air I breathed.

Then my dad died when I was seventeen.

Overnight, the living-room church died with him. I didn't just lose a father—I lost a world. I had no choice but to walk into traditional churches next. Good churches. Sincere churches. Churches full of people who loved Jesus.

But something was missing.

I couldn't always name it, but I felt it like a low-grade ache. The programs multiplied. The buildings grew. The politics crept in. Somewhere along the way, apprenticeship to Jesus quietly gave way to managing institutions, curating experiences, and measuring success by attendance and budgets.

And I joined right in.

For decades, I played the game faithfully. I showed up. I served. I taught. I led. From the outside, it looked like devotion. On the inside, I was slowly starving. I was busy building small religious kingdoms while the life Jesus promised felt farther and farther away.

Twenty years after my dad was gone, I met a teacher named Nick.

Talking with Nick felt like picking up sentences my dad had started decades earlier and never got to finish. The same fire. The same clarity. The same unshakable conviction that the kingdom of God is not a metaphor or a future reward—but a present reality ordinary people can live in.

Nick pointed me to a quiet philosopher-theologian named Dallas Willard.

I bought *The Divine Conspiracy* expecting another smart Christian book. Instead, it felt like someone handed me a transcript of every late-night conversation I never got to have with my dad. Same heartbeat. Same confidence. Same insistence that Jesus meant what He said—that eternal life is available now, and that discipleship is not optional if we actually want it.

It took me three stubborn years to let that truth sink in.

Three years of reading every Willard book. Watching scratchy early-2000s lectures on YouTube. Circling, resisting, arguing, and eventually surrendering. Not to new ideas—but to the ones I'd lost along the way.

This book is the shortcut I wish someone had handed me the week after my dad's funeral.

It's the gold I mined out of dense pages, long regrets, and slow repentance—boiled down into plain language for the people I love most. Written from three years of notes, late nights, and unfinished conversations finally brought to completion.

If you grew up watching adults miss the very thing Jesus came to give, this book is for you.

The kingdom is still at hand.

My dad would have loved this conversation. I'm just finishing it for him.

"Grace writes straight with crooked lines."

I first wrote that in *Letters to Mitchell*, and it's still the only way I can explain how this book finally happened. None of this followed a straight path. But grace has a way of turning detours into directions—and of finishing conversations we thought were lost.

PROLOGUE

This book is for you.

If no one else ever reads it, that's fine. You are the reason I'm writing.

I look at you and feel two things at once.

First, pride. The kind that almost hurts. You are thoughtful, perceptive, and honest in ways my generation often wasn't. You care about what's real. You smell hypocrisy from a mile away. You refuse to pretend.

Second, fear.

Many of you have walked away from Jesus. Others are still nearby but barely holding on. And I'm convinced it's not because you rejected Him—but because the version of Christianity you grew up watching didn't work.

It didn't touch your anxiety.
It didn't quiet the noise in your head.
It didn't feel like Good News.

We gave you youth group games and fog machines.
We gave you sermons that scolded more than they healed.
We gave you rules, politics, and Christian slogans.

We never gave you the kingdom.

I'm old enough now to know I don't have decades left to fix this in passing conversations or family dinners. So I'm putting everything I wish I had taught you—and everything I wish someone had taught me when I was twenty—into a book short enough to read in a weekend.

If I'm wrong about all of this, laugh about it at my funeral.

But if I'm right, this may be the most important inheritance I could ever leave you.

The Crisis We Can No Longer Ignore

What I see in our family, I now see everywhere.

Most Christians today love Jesus sincerely—but they don't know how to live in His kingdom.

They were taught how to attend church.
They were taught how to behave.
They were taught how to believe the right things.

They were rarely taught how to live the kind of life Jesus actually offered.

That gap—the distance between what Jesus promised and what most believers experience—is quietly suffocating an entire generation.

We have churches full of people who are:

- anxious but faithful

- exhausted but committed

- constantly connected but deeply lonely

- spiritually sincere but practically powerless

They believe in heaven.
They don't know how to live with God today.

They believe the gospel forgives sins.
They were never shown that it also makes people free.

They believe Jesus is Savior.
They were never taught that He is also the smartest Person who ever lived—and the best Teacher we could ever follow.

Somewhere along the way, the church traded the message Jesus preached—*"The kingdom of God is at hand"*—for something smaller, thinner, and easier to manage.

We replaced apprenticeship with attendance.
Transformation with tips.
Kingdom life with religious activity.

And people are starving.

What Jesus Actually Brought

Jesus did not come to start a religion.

He came to announce and demonstrate a new kind of life—His life—now available to ordinary people in ordinary moments.

The kingdom of God is the range of God's effective will: where what God wants done is actually being done.

And Jesus' earth-shaking announcement was simple:

That life is now within your reach.

Not after you die.
Not after decades of trying harder.
Right now.

This is the gospel He preached.
This is the gospel the early church lived.
This is the message modern Christianity quietly misplaced.

Why This Book Exists

In my lifetime, no one explained this more clearly—or lived it more convincingly—than Dallas Willard.

Willard didn't invent anything new. He cleared away religious fog so we could see Jesus again. Through his writing and his life, he showed that:

- salvation is more than sin-management

- discipleship is more than church involvement

- grace is not opposed to effort, but to earning

- kingdom life is possible in the middle of jobs, diapers, exams, and grief

But Willard wrote for serious students.

A new generation needs the same fire in language that fits the world you actually live in.

That's why this book exists.

An Invitation

What follows is not a commentary.
It's not an argument.

It's an invitation.

An invitation to step into the life Jesus offered—the with-God life that starts now and never ends.

By the time you close the last page, you'll know three things clearly:

- what Jesus actually meant when He said *"the kingdom"*

- why your life does not have to stay stuck the way it is

- how to begin training—not just trying—your way into freedom, joy, and power that last

All I'm asking is one weekend of your life.

The kingdom of God is still at hand.

Let's step into it—together.

I love you,
Dad / Granddad

Chapter 1

THE OFFER STILL STANDS

There is a kind of life on this planet most Christians have never tasted.

Not the life of perfect circumstances.
Not the life of never screwing up.

The life Jesus lived—and the life He said anyone could live who simply followed Him.

A life where

peace is the default setting, not a rare mood

joy shows up even when the bank account is empty

fear no longer gets a vote

loving impossible people feels natural, not heroic

you walk through ordinary days with the quiet, unshakable certainty that God is with you, in you, for you

Jesus called this "eternal life."

Not just endless duration.
Life powered by the age to come—available right now.

Most of us were told eternal life begins the moment you die.
Jesus said it begins the moment you trust Him enough to follow Him.

He never once said, "Believe some facts about Me and I'll punch your ticket to heaven."
He said, "Follow Me—and I will give you the life you've been looking for your whole life."

That offer never expired.

It didn't expire when the church got organized.
It didn't expire when Christianity became an empire.
It didn't expire when we turned it into fog machines and political voting blocs.

The offer still stands.

Today.
For you.

In the middle of your actual life—your actual anxiety, your actual phone addiction, your actual loneliness, your actual questions.

Jesus is still saying the same thing He said to fishermen, tax collectors, and prostitutes two thousand years ago:

"Come with Me.
I'll teach you how to live the life you only glimpse in your best moments."

Most people never take Him up on it.

Not because they don't love Jesus.
Because no one ever showed them it was actually possible.

This book is that demonstration.

By the time you finish, you'll know exactly how to step into the life He's been offering all along.

Not in theory.
Not after you "get your act together."

Starting this week.

The offer still stands.
The only question left is: will you take it?

Chapter 2

JESUS DROPPED A MIC, NOT A RELIGION

Open your Bible app and search "kingdom of God" in the Gospels.
You'll get over a hundred hits.

Now search "go to heaven when you die."
You'll get zero.

Not a single time did Jesus say it.

That's not a small detail.
That's the whole difference between the gospel Jesus preached and the one most of us heard growing up.

Here's what Jesus actually walked around saying, everywhere He went:

"The kingdom of the heavens is at hand."
"The kingdom of God has come near."
"The kingdom is in your midst."

He said it so often the writers got tired of etching the full sentence and just wrote, "He went on preaching the gospel of the kingdom."

That was His headline.
That was His mission statement.
That was the Good News.

So what is the kingdom?

It's not a place.
It's not "heaven later."

It's the range of God's effective will.

Wherever what God wants done is actually getting done—that's the kingdom.

When someone is forgiven, healed, delivered, restored, or simply filled with unexplainable peace in the middle of chaos, the kingdom just showed up.

And Jesus' entire message was this:

"That way of life, that power, that reality is now available to everyone who wants it.
No waiting period.
No entrance exam.
No 'clean yourself up first.'
Right now.
Reach out and take it."

He proved it by doing kingdom stuff in front of everyone:

- Demons ran.

- Storms shut up.

- Blind people saw.

- Dead girls woke up.

- Guilty women walked free without shame.

Then He turned to regular people—fishermen, tax collectors, teenagers—and said, "You do it too."

And they did.

That's the gospel Jesus preached.

Somehow we turned it into:
"Pray this prayer, try not to sin too much, show up on Sundays, and hope you make it to heaven when you die."

We took the most explosive announcement in history and neutered it into a religious loyalty program.

Jesus didn't come to start Christianity.
He came to launch a kingdom invasion of planet Earth

and invite anyone who's tired of the old way to join Him.

The same kingdom He brought is still breaking in today.

I've seen it.
I've tasted it.

And I've watched twenty-somethings who were done with church light up the moment they realized Jesus wasn't offering them a religion.

He was offering them a revolution.

The announcement hasn't changed.
The kingdom of God is still at hand.

Question is: are we brave enough to drop the religion and grab the kingdom?

Chapter 3

CONSUMER CHRISTIANITY IS BANKRUPT

Let's not kid ourselves.

Most of us didn't grow up in churches that taught the kingdom.
We grew up in churches that sold a product.

Different branding, same transaction:
You give God your Sundays, your tithe, your vote, your youth-group attendance, your not-cussing-too-much.

In return you get guilt relief, a get-out-of-hell-free card, warm feelings during the slow song, and the vague hope that someday everything will finally be okay.

We turned the faith into the spiritual version of Amazon Prime: pay the membership fee, click a few buttons, get heaven delivered.

It worked great... until it didn't.

Because eventually you hit a week—or a year—when the worship playlist doesn't touch the panic attacks, the marriage still implodes, the guilt keeps coming back, and heaven feels a million miles away from Monday morning.

That's when you discover the brutal truth:
Consumer Christianity is spiritually bankrupt.

It has zero power for the life you're actually living.

Jesus never offered a product.
He offered a life.

He never asked for customers.
He asked for followers who would lose their lives to find them.

Customers want maximum benefits for minimum cost.
Followers want to become like the Master, whatever it costs.

Consumer Christianity keeps you weak on purpose—it needs you coming back for the next conference, the next album, the next emotional high.

Kingdom Christianity makes you dangerous—it trains you to live with the same power, love, and self-control Jesus had, right in the middle of this broken world.

I fell for the consumer version too.

Decades of paying my dues, collecting the stickers, waiting for the upgrade that never came.

Then I finally heard what Jesus actually said:
"Whoever wants to save their life will lose it,
but whoever loses their life for Me and for the gospel will find it."

Translation: stop trying to get something out of Jesus. Start giving your whole life to Him.

That's when you finally get the life you were trying to buy.

Consumer Christianity is bankrupt.
The kingdom is solvent, overflowing, and free to anyone willing to stop shopping and start following.

Your move.

Chapter 4

APPRENTICE, NOT FAN

Jesus never asked anyone to be a Christian.

He never asked anyone to be a worshipper, a church member, or a "believer" in the modern sense.

He used two words, over and over:

"Follow Me."

That's it.

Two words that changed fishermen into world-changers and prostitutes into saints.

Not "admire Me."
Not "agree with Me."
Not "sing about Me."

Follow Me.

In Jesus' day, that phrase had a very specific meaning everyone understood.

A rabbi would walk the dusty roads, teaching, healing, living fully alive.

Young men who saw something different in him would beg to become his *talmidim*—his apprentices.

If the rabbi thought they had potential, he'd say, "Come, follow me."

That meant:
leave your nets, your tax booth, your old life.
Move in close.
Watch everything I do.
Listen to everything I say.
Copy me until my way of being human becomes your way of being human.

It wasn't school.
It was life-on-life transformation.

Jesus looked at the same kind of ordinary, messed-up people and used the exact same invitation:

"Follow Me."

He still uses it today.

But somewhere along the way we downgraded the invitation.

We turned "Follow Me" into "Like Me from a safe distance."

We became fans instead of apprentices.

Fans cheer on game day (Sunday).
Apprentices train every day.

Fans consume content.
Apprentices imitate a Master.

Fans want autographs and selfies.
Apprentices want to become like the One they follow.

Fans say, "I love Jesus."
Apprentices say, "I'm with Jesus—wherever, whatever, however long it takes."

Here's the difference it makes in real life:

Fans still lose their temper in traffic.
Apprentices slowly grow the same patience they see in Jesus.

Fans binge Netflix to numb the pain.
Apprentices learn to sit with Jesus in silence until the pain loses its power.

Fans post Bible verses while secretly scrolling porn.
Apprentices let Jesus rewire their desires from the inside out.

Fans quit when it gets hard.
Apprentices expected it to be hard—and signed up anyway.

Jesus never promised that following Him would be easy.
He promised it would work.

He promised that if we stay close enough, long enough, His life will rub off on us.

That's still the deal.

No super-Christian tier required.
Just ordinary people who decide to move in close and copy the Master.

So here's the question every one of my kids and grandkids has to answer eventually:
Are you a fan, or are you an apprentice?

Because Jesus is still walking the road, still doing kingdom stuff, still inviting ordinary people to drop everything and follow.

He's looking at you right now.

And He's still saying the exact same two words:

"Follow Me."

Chapter 5

The Curriculum of Christ

Most of us were taught that the Sermon on the Mount is a beautiful but impossible ideal, like spiritual Mount Everest: nice to look at, deadly to climb.

We turned Jesus' most famous sermon into a guilt trip:

"Blessed are the pure in heart... yeah, I'm out."
"Love your enemies... hard pass."
"Don't worry about tomorrow... tell that to my credit card."

Pastors preach it, then quietly add, "Of course, we all fail at this; that's why we need grace."

That's exactly backward.

Jesus didn't give the Sermon on the Mount to show us how miserably we fail.

He gave it as the syllabus for kingdom life; the description of what normal looks like when a human being is fully plugged into God's kingdom.

It's not the entrance exam.
It's the graduation photo.

When someone is truly living in the kingdom (when God's rule has full access to their heart, mind, body, and habits), this is what naturally shows up:

- They're gentle when they could dominate.

- They stay kind when everything says retaliate.

- They're free from anxiety even when the world is on fire.

- Their sexual desires come under new management.

- Their words carry weight because they mean what they say.

- They love people who hate them without faking it.

That's not superhero Christianity.
That's baseline kingdom humanity.

Jesus isn't mocking us with an unreachable standard. He's showing us the target, then spending the rest of His life teaching us how to hit it.

Think of it like learning to drive.

No driving instructor hands you the keys on day one and says, "Obey every traffic law perfectly or you fail forever."

That would be insane.

Instead they say, "This is what good driving looks like. Now get in; we're going to practice until it becomes second nature."

Jesus did the same thing.

The Sermon on the Mount is the picture on the box of the puzzle.
The rest of the Gospels are Him sitting at the table with us, helping us put the pieces together.

He knows we'll stall the car, run a few red lights, and maybe back into a mailbox or two.

But He also knows that if we keep training with Him (not just reading the manual, not just watching videos, but actually driving with the Master in the passenger seat), we'll get there.

The Sermon on the Mount is not there to condemn you.
It's there to show you who you're becoming.

And the crazy part?

You don't have to wait until you're "good enough" to start living it.

You start living it the moment you pull your chair up next to Jesus and say, "Teach me."

Because the same power that raised Christ from the dead is the same power that can raise your anger-management skills, your porn habit, your anxiety, and your bitterness from the dead too.

The curriculum still works.
Class is in session.
Your Rabbi is waiting.

Chapter 6

THE BEATITUDES—THE KINGDOM'S OPEN DOORS

We all know the Beatitudes.

They open the Sermon on the Mount with lines that feel stitched on pillows or captioned under mountain sunsets:

Blessed are the poor in spirit...
Blessed are those who mourn...
Blessed are the meek...

We've heard them at weddings, funerals, and on coffee mugs. We've nodded in sermons. We've treated them like soft inspirational music—beautiful, but safely distant from real life.

That's a mistake.

Jesus wasn't handing out poetic encouragement or virtues for spiritual superstars. He was naming the exact places where the kingdom of heaven **breaks in**.

The Beatitudes are not the finish line.
They are the starting line.

Jesus begins His greatest teaching by saying, in effect:

If your life feels shattered, hollow, aching, or utterly spent—congratulations. You're standing in the precise spot where God's rule breaks through.

That one shift changes everything.

The Kingdom Is Not for the Put-Together

Most of us secretly read the Beatitudes as a to-do list:

Be poorer in spirit.
Be more mournful.
Be meeker.
Be merciful.

No wonder they feel exhausting. Who wants to manufacture brokenness?

But Jesus isn't commanding us to fake these states. He's blessing the people who already find themselves there.

The Beatitudes are not instructions.
They are announcements of grace.

The kingdom doesn't belong to the impressive, the confident, or the spiritually polished. It belongs to the ones who have run out of pretense.

The kingdom is not climbed.
It is received by surrender.

Blessed Are the Poor in Spirit

"Blessed are the poor in spirit, for theirs is the kingdom of heaven."

Not *will be.* **Is.** Present tense.

This is first for a reason. "Poor in spirit" means spiritual bankruptcy—you've exhausted your own fixes, your self-help, your performance. No more bargaining. No more faking strength.

The addict finally out of excuses.
The parent staring at the ceiling at 3 a.m., answers gone.
The high-achiever who "made it" and still feels like a fraud inside.

Jesus says: that emptiness isn't disqualification. It's your invitation.

The kingdom arrives not when you're strong enough, but when you're empty enough for God to fill.

Blessed Are Those Who Mourn

"Blessed are those who mourn, for they will be comforted."

Not performative tears or tidy public sadness. Real mourning—the raw ache that the world is broken, that life isn't what it should be.

The spouse who walked away.
The diagnosis that stole breath.
The dream that died quietly while everyone else moved on.

Jesus doesn't rush past the pain with "cheer up" or "silver lining." He steps into it:

I will meet you here. I will comfort you—not by erasing the wound, but by entering it until it becomes a doorway to deeper life.

Some of our clearest glimpses of God come not in triumph, but in tears watered by His presence.

Blessed Are the Meek

"Blessed are the meek, for they will inherit the earth."

Meekness isn't weakness or spinelessness. It's power that chooses not to dominate.

The colleague who could win the argument with one cutting reply—but chooses silence for peace.
The leader who could seize control—but trusts God's timing instead.

In a culture obsessed with hustle, self-promotion, and winning at all costs, meekness looks like losing. Jesus calls it wisdom.

The aggressive **burn out**; the meek endure.
And endurance inherits what force can never hold.

Blessed Are Those Who Hunger and Thirst for Righteousness

"Blessed are those who hunger and thirst for righteousness, for they will be filled."

This isn't hunger for rules or moral perfection. It's a deep, restless longing for things to be set right—with God, with others, within your own soul.

If hypocrisy (yours or the world's) keeps you awake, if you ache for wholeness you can't manufacture—Jesus says that hunger isn't a flaw to fix.

It's proof you're alive to the kingdom.

The world offers quick fixes: success, distraction, approval. They satisfy for a moment.

The kingdom fills deeply. Finally. Forever.

Blessed Are the Merciful

"Blessed are the merciful, for they will be shown mercy."

Mercy isn't pretending wrong didn't happen. It's refusing to let wrong have the last word.

It's dropping the ledger of grievances.
Choosing release over resentment.
Grace over scorekeeping.

In the kingdom, mercy isn't soft—it's liberating.

What you grip tightens its grip on you.
What you release sets you free.

Mercy doesn't excuse harm; it dismantles its power.

Blessed Are the Pure in Heart

"Blessed are the pure in heart, for they will see God."

Purity isn't flawless morality. It's single-minded focus—a heart no longer split between God and a thousand distractions.

The pure in heart aren't perfect; they're undivided.

When your attention is aimed in one direction, God starts showing up everywhere: in ordinary conversations, in interruptions, in suffering, in silence.

Seeing God isn't a prize for achievement.
It's the natural result of looking in the right direction.

Blessed Are the Peacemakers

"Blessed are the peacemakers, for they will be called children of God."

Not peacekeepers who dodge conflict at any cost. Peacemakers who step into fractured places with courage and humility.

In divided families, polarized workplaces, broken friendships—this work is expensive. It requires swallowing pride, listening first, forgiving ahead of time.

But it reveals family resemblance.

This is what God does—bridging impossible divides. When we do it, people see Him in us.

Blessed Are the Persecuted

"Blessed are those who are persecuted because of righteousness, for theirs is the kingdom of heaven."

Following Jesus can cost you approval, advancement, comfort—even safety. Jesus doesn't sugarcoat it.

But He promises this: opposition doesn't mean you've missed the kingdom. Often it means you've entered it.

Again: **theirs is the kingdom.** Present tense.

The Door Stands Wide Open

These are not impossible ideals for elite believers. They are wide-open doors into the kingdom.

Jesus begins His most famous sermon by ensuring no one is left outside—especially the ones who feel most unworthy.

The kingdom isn't reserved for the impressive.
It's for the honest.

If you're tired, grieving, empty, overlooked, or just done pretending—listen closely:

You are not disqualified.
You are invited.

Step through.

The kingdom is waiting—not someday, not after you clean up your act, but **right now**.

Once you're in, everything changes.

Not later.
Now.

Chapter 7

YOUR SECRET LIFE IS THE REAL ONE

Jesus never fixed the outside first.
He always went straight for the heart.

"You've heard 'Don't murder'—but I say if contempt lives in your heart, you're already on trial."

"You've heard 'Don't commit adultery'—but I say if lust owns your imagination, you've already crossed the line."

Why? Because God isn't impressed with behavior management.
He's obsessed with what's happening beneath the surface.

Your secret life—the thoughts you rehearse, the fantasies you nurture, the quiet resentments you feed, the fears you whisper when no one's listening—that's the real you.

That's where the kingdom either takes root or gets choked out.

We live in a world that only grades the highlight reel.

As long as the Instagram looks perfect and the family photo is framed, we think we're good.

Jesus calls the bluff.

What happens in secret always leaks out eventually.

A nursed thought becomes a spoken word.
A repeated word becomes a habit.
A habit becomes a character.
And character is destiny.

The kingdom doesn't begin with better rules.
It begins with a renovated heart.

How?

Not by trying harder to be good.
By opening the vault and letting Jesus in.

Invite Him into the anger you replay on the drive home.
Invite Him into the lust you click on.
Invite Him into the worry that keeps you awake at 3 a.m.
Invite Him into the greed, the envy, the pride.

He doesn't come to shame you.
He comes to clean house—gently, thoroughly, permanently.

I lived decades of outward success while greed and pride quietly ruled the back rooms of my heart.

The day I finally cracked the door and said, "Come in here too," everything changed.

Not overnight. But steadily.

The overflow got kinder. The peace got deeper. The joy got real.

Your secret life is the real one.
Don't hide it.
Hand it over.

The kingdom starts there.

So here's the scary, freeing truth I wish someone had told me thirty years sooner:

Jesus isn't waiting for you to clean up the mess yourself.
He's waiting for you to stop trying harder and start training with Him.

Turn the page.
Class is about to begin.

Chapter 8

STOP TRYING HARDER (START TRAINING)

You've tried. We all have.

That burst of resolve after a convicting sermon or a rock-bottom moment: "This time, I'm really going to change."

No more yelling at the kids. No more doom-scrolling till midnight. No more skipping prayer because "life's too busy."

You grit your teeth, set the alarm earlier, download the app, tell a friend for accountability.

And for a week—maybe two—it works.

Then the old habits creep back. The alarm gets snoozed. The app gets deleted. The friend gets an awkward "yeah, about that" text.

And you're left feeling like a failure. Again.

Here's the good news: It's not your fault. Not entirely.

The problem isn't your willpower. It's your method.

We've been sold a lie:
that spiritual growth happens by trying harder. By sheer determination. By bootstrapping your way to holiness.

Jesus never taught that.
Neither did Paul, or any apostle.

They taught something radically different: training. Not trying.

Dallas Willard nailed it: **"Grace is not opposed to effort; it's opposed to earning."**

Effort is essential. But the right kind of effort.

Trying is like sprinting a marathon—you burn out, then crash.
Training is like preparing for the race: steady, strategic, sustainable.

You build capacity over time. You practice in low-stakes ways until the big moments feel natural.

Think about it.

No athlete "tries harder" to win the Olympics. They train: reps in the gym, laps in the pool, film study, nutrition tweaks. Day after day. Until excellence becomes automatic.

Jesus invites us to do the same for kingdom living.

The Sermon on the Mount isn't a list of "try harder" commands. It's a training manual.

"Love your enemies?" Train for it.
"Don't worry?" Practice it.
"Be perfect as your Father is perfect?" Not instant magic—progressive formation.

So how do we shift from trying to training?

It starts with this mindset flip:

You're not fixing a broken you.
You're cooperating with a loving God who's already at work reshaping you from the inside out.

Grace fuels the training. Not guilt.

Here's the kingdom training playbook—simple, doable steps to build the life Jesus described. No religious jargon. Just real transformation for your real week.

Identify the Target:

Pick one area from the Sermon that's kicking your butt. Anxiety? Anger? Lust?

Don't tackle everything. Jesus didn't overwhelm His apprentices.

Start small: "This month, I'm training in peace."

Indirect Effort First:

Direct trying often backfires (e.g., "Stop worrying!" just makes you worry about worrying).

Train indirectly. For anxiety, practice gratitude journaling—not to force calm, but to rewire your focus.

Willard called this "off-spot training"—build the muscle sideways.

Build Habits, Not Heroics:

Heroes pull all-nighters. Trainees build routines.

Set a 5-minute silence sit each morning. Not to "be spiritual," but to train your mind to rest in God.

Stack it on coffee time. Consistency compounds.

Expect Resistance (and Grace for It):

Your flesh will fight back. That's normal. Paul called it "the law of sin" in your members.

Don't quit—adjust. Missed a day? No shame. Grace says: "Get back in the gym."

Track progress, not perfection.

Community as Coach:

Apprentices didn't go solo.

Find a few trusted friends—not for accountability guilt trips, but for encouragement.

Share wins. Ask: "How's your training going?"

Church small groups could be training camps, not just chat sessions.

Rest as Rep:

Training includes recovery.

Sabbath isn't lazy—it's strategic. Jesus withdrew often.

Burnout isn't holy.

Train in rest: One day a week, no screens, no striving. Let God restore.

Measure by Fruit, Not Feelings:

Don't judge by "Did I feel spiritual today?"

Ask: "Am I responding more like Jesus?"

Less reactive anger? Deeper joy in chaos? That's the win. Fruit takes seasons to grow.

I lived the "try harder" life for years. New Year's resolutions. Spiritual diets. Boom and bust.

Then I discovered training through Willard's writings.

Started small: Training in listening before speaking. Practiced in meetings, with my wife, even in my head during drives.

At first, awkward. Now? Natural.

Conflicts de-escalate. Relationships deepen.

Grace did the heavy lifting—I just showed up for practice.

You're not condemned for failing at "trying."

You're invited to train with the Master Coach.

He knows your weaknesses. He celebrates your reps.

Stop trying harder. Start training smarter.

The kingdom life you've envied? It's built one practice at a time.

Your session starts now.
Lace up.

Chapter 9

SPIRITUAL DISCIPLINES WITHOUT THE RELIGIOUS WEIRDNESS

You've heard the term "spiritual disciplines" and maybe pictured monks in robes chanting at dawn or ascetics starving in caves.

Sounds intense. Sounds irrelevant. Sounds... weird.

But strip away the religious baggage, and spiritual disciplines are just smart training tools.

They're the gym equipment for your soul.

The practices Jesus Himself used to stay connected to the Father amid chaos.

Dallas Willard described them as **"activities within our power that enable us to do what we cannot do by direct effort."**

They're not about earning God's love (that's already yours).
They're about positioning yourself to receive it.

To let kingdom life flow through you naturally.

Jesus fasted—not to impress God, but to sharpen His focus.
He withdrew to solitude—not to escape people, but to recharge for them.
He studied Scripture—not as homework, but as fuel.

These aren't for super-Christians.

They're for burned-out baristas, stressed parents, scrolling students—anyone tired of white-knuckling faith.

The goal? **Freedom.**

Joy that sticks. Peace that holds. Love that lasts.

Without the weirdness.

Let's repackage five core disciplines for your actual life. No cloaks required. Just willingness to experiment.

Think of them as apps for apprenticeship—download, practice, upgrade your OS.

Silence: The Antidote to Noise Addiction

Our world is a non-stop podcast of notifications, opinions, and inner chatter.

Jesus often "went away to a solitary place" to pray.

Training move: Start with 5 minutes a day. Phone in airplane mode. Sit. Breathe. Let thoughts come and go without judging.

Don't force "holy thoughts"—just be quiet with God.

Pro tip: Do it during your commute or before bed.

Over time? The mental static fades. Decisions clarify. Anxiety dials down.

I've turned car rides into silence sessions; now, road rage is ancient history.

Solitude: Reclaiming Your Inner Room

Not loneliness—intentional alone time to detox from people-pleasing.

Jesus slipped away from crowds, even disciples, to realign.

For you: Block 30 minutes weekly. No agenda. Walk in the park, journal random thoughts, or stare at a wall.

Ask: "God, what's stirring in me?"

It's weird at first—your brain rebels like a toddler without their paci.

But persist. Solitude reveals the you beneath the masks.

It rebuilt my marriage: alone time helped me process resentment before it spilled out.

Fasting: Beyond the Diet Hype

Skip the intermittent fasting trends.

Biblical fasting skips food (or screens, shopping) to hunger for God instead.

Jesus fasted 40 days; it tuned Him to the Father's voice.

Modern twist: Start small—a meal, or a day without social media.

Use the "hunger pangs" (literal or digital) as prompts to pray: "God, fill this space."

Not punishment—it's recalibration.

Frees you from "hangry" impulses or doom-scrolling.

I fasted from news once; gained back hours and a calmer heart.

Bonus: Clarity on big decisions surges.

Study: Feasting on Wisdom, Not Just Skimming

Not Bible trivia—immersive soaking in truth.

Jesus quoted Scripture effortlessly because He lived in it.

Your version: Pick a Gospel passage. Read slow. Journal: "What jumps out? How does this hit my life?"

Use apps like Bible Gateway.

Go deep on one verse over cramming chapters.

Willard said study transforms your mind's "default settings."

It did for me: Studying "do not worry" rewired my financial insecurity into trust.

Pro move: Pair with a podcast like The Bible Project for context without overwhelm.

Celebration: Joy as Rebellion

Sounds fun, right? It is. But it's a discipline because our culture defaults to complaint.

Jesus turned water to wine at a party—He celebrated life.

Practice: Weekly, list gratitudes out loud.

Throw small feasts for no reason—tacos with friends, dancing to dumb playlists.

Make joy intentional amid grind.

It combats burnout like nothing else.

My family started "best part of your day"—sharing highs of the day over the drive home.

Shifted our rides from tense to thankful.

These aren't checkboxes. They're experiments.

Try one this week. Adjust as needed.

If it feels forced, pivot—God meets you in the mess, not the method.

Remember: Disciplines aren't the point. Jesus is.

They just clear the path so you can walk with Him easier.

I've watched skeptics try silence and say, "Whoa, God's voice got louder."

Burned-out parents fast from screens and rediscover play.

Students study and find purpose amid midterms.

Without the weirdness. Just real change.

The kingdom isn't abstract theology. It's practiced reality.

These tools make it tangible.

Pick one. Start today.

Your freer self is waiting.

Chapter 10

LIVING THE KINGDOM IN A BURNOUT CULTURE

You're exhausted. I know.

Our culture runs on burnout fuel: notifications, comparison, hustle porn, and the lie that more is always better.

Money, sex, power, ambition, social media—five traps perfectly designed to own you.

Kingdom living isn't escape.
It's invasion.

Jesus walked straight into parties, tax booths, and Roman-occupied streets and showed that God's rule can redeem every single trap—right where you live.

Money → from master to servant
Sex → from impulse to fierce intimacy
Power → from control to foot-washing surrender
Ambition → from ladder-climbing to kingdom-build-

ing
Social media → from scroll to soul

These aren't new rules.
They're training upgrades.

Pick one trap this week.
Invite the King in.
Watch what He does with surrendered ground.

I've stumbled in every single one.
I still do.

But every time I hand one over, I wake up lighter, love deeper, live bolder.

Burnout culture promises everything and delivers exhaustion.

Kingdom culture delivers everything burnout stole: rest, purpose, joy that lasts.

Your life doesn't have to stay stuck.

Upgrade to kingdom OS.

It runs smoother.
It never crashes.
It was made for this world—and the next.

Start today.
Pick one trap.
Let the invasion begin.

Chapter 11

THE CHURCH AS TRAINING CAMP, NOT MUSEUM

Church feels cringe sometimes.

Fog machines. Skinny jeans. Surface-level small talk.

You've been hurt, ignored, or just bored stiff.

Maybe you walked away. Maybe you're hanging on by a thread.

I get it.

We turned church into a museum: pretty artifacts, Sunday tours optional.

Jesus built a movement.

The early church wasn't a weekly show.

It was boot camp.

Messy, real, life-on-life.

They ate, prayed, confessed, shared everything, and turned the world upside down—not because they had better programs, but because they trained together.

We need that again.

Isolation kills growth.
Community accelerates it—even when it's awkward.

So reframe it:
Church isn't a museum to visit.
It's training camp to sweat in.

Show up ready to practice, not just watch.

Confess the mess (safely).
Serve like your character depends on it (it does).

Find a squad that's actually training, not posing.

If your church is dead, don't just complain—coach it back to life.

If it's toxic, leave gracefully and find (or start) a healthier camp.

I quit "church" in my thirties. I was lonely.

Then I found a few people who wanted to train, not perform.

We started practicing together albeit over the phone mostly.

Wounds healed. Faith caught fire.

Our homes and jobs became kingdom outposts.

You need the church—not the museum kind.

The camp kind.

Where apprentices stumble, sweat, and stand together.

Find your squad.
Or start one.

The King is calling roll.
Answer up.

Chapter 12

THE UNHURRIED REVOLUTION

You've made it this far. One weekend, as promised.

But the kingdom isn't a book you finish—it's a life you begin.

And here's the plot twist: You don't have to storm the gates or go viral to change the world.

Jesus didn't.

He launched the greatest revolution in history with a dozen nobodies, quiet conversations, and a cross that looked like failure.

No TED Talks. No social media campaigns. No power grabs.

Just unhurried faithfulness.

Person by person. Moment by moment.

Dallas Willard called it "the conspiracy of goodness"—ordinary people living kingdom life so consistently that evil loses its footing.

Not through noise. Through nearness.

The unhurried revolution isn't flashy. It's subversive.

It spreads like yeast in dough—slow, invisible, inevitable.

In a hurry-up-and-hustle world, this feels counterintuitive.

But look at history:

The early church outlasted Rome not by armies, but by loving enemies, caring for plagues, and living free amid chains.

Today? The same power hums.

A few kingdom people—apprentices like you—quietly changing everything.

Your anxiety eases? **That's revolution in your brain.**
Your marriage mends? **Revolution in your home.**
Your workplace witnesses kindness amid cutthroat?
Revolution in the economy.

It scales.

One transformed heart sparks another.

No rush. Just ripple.

So how do you join?

Not by adding more to your plate.
By subtracting hurry.

Embedding kingdom rhythms.

Living as if eternity starts now—because it does.

Here's the unhurried playbook. Not a to-do list. A way of being.

Breathe it in. Live it out. Watch the world shift.

Embrace the Slow Kingdom Pace

Culture screams "faster."
Jesus walked—literally.

Training: Build margins. Say no to good things for God's things.

Schedule unhurried time: A meal without phones. A walk without podcasts.

Willard lived this—simple routines, profound impact.

I rushed for decades; slowing down multiplied my influence.

Revolution starts in rest: Unhurried souls outlast frantic empires.

Invest in Hidden Acts

Big changes come from small obediences no one sees.

Pray for the jerk boss in secret.
Forgive the family grudge quietly.
Give anonymously.

Jesus said the Father rewards these. Why?

They rewire you for purity, not performance.

In my life, private prayers shifted public battles.

The unhurried revolution thrives underground—roots before fruits.

Cultivate Kingdom Friendships

Revolutions need allies.

Not crowds—confidants.

Find 2–3 apprentices to train with: Weekly check-ins on disciplines, honest shares on failures.

Jesus had His three (Peter, James, John).
Willard mentored quietly.

My circle? We confess, encourage, serve together.

No fanfare. Just faithfulness.

These bonds outpace solo efforts, sparking mini-revolutions in neighborhoods.

Engage Culture Without Enslaving to It

Don't isolate—invade.

At work, embody integrity amid shortcuts.
On socials, post truth amid trolls.
In politics, vote kingdom values without idolizing parties.

Jesus dined with sinners, flipped tables when needed.

Training: Daily discern: "Does this align with love, justice, peace?"

I've navigated divides this way; quiet witness wins more than loud arguments.

Expect Opposition (and Outlove It)

Revolutions ruffle feathers.

You'll face mockery, misunderstanding, maybe loss.

Jesus promised: "In this world you will have trouble. But take heart—I have overcome."

Unhurried response: Bless persecutors. Serve enemies.

Willard faced critics gracefully.

In my story, opposition tested my training—love disarmed it.

The kingdom advances not by force, but by unconquerable goodness.

Measure by Mustard Seeds, Not Mountains

Forget metrics. Kingdom growth is seed-sized:

A kind word plants hope.
A forgiven debt frees a soul.

Jesus' parables promise: Small starts yield massive harvests.

Track eternity: "Did I love like Him today?"

My grandkids see this in me now—not perfection, but progress.

That's the inheritance.

This is the gospel of the kingdom.

Not fire insurance for later.
Life with God now.

Unhurried. Unstoppable.

You've tasted it in these pages.

But tasting isn't enough.

Step in. Train daily. Join the conspiracy.

I'm not wrong.

This changes everything.

For you. For us. For the world.

I love you,
Dad / Granddaddy

(And if this sparked something, pass it on. The revolution needs recruits.)

Epilogue: The Inheritance That Lasts

You've closed the book.
But the kingdom doesn't end here.
It begins.

Some of you are already neck-deep in Dallas's books—good, keep going.

This little book isn't a replacement; it's a gateway drug.

When you're ready for the full-weight glory, open *The Divine Conspiracy* chapter 2 and *Renovation of the Heart* chapter 5.

You'll recognize the same fire that's been burning in you since page one.

I just wanted you to taste it first in your own language.

I wrote these pages picturing you on the couch, coffee getting cold, eyes lighting up as the pieces finally click.

That's my prayer.

Not that you agree with every word.
But that you taste the life Jesus died to give you—the unhurried, unbreakable kind—and never settle for less again.

Looking back, the crisis that broke my heart (and yours) wasn't just the church's fault.
It was mine.

I lived faithful but frantic for too long.

Programs over presence.
Belief over becoming.

Now, at this stage of life, I see the fruit:

Dinner tables with no agenda, just scars and grace.
Late-night phone calls where anxiety gets prayed into peace.
Quiet moments when the kingdom breaks in and we all know it.

Those are the wins.

That's the inheritance.

Dallas passed the torch quietly.

I'm passing it to you the same way.

Not as a burden.
As a gift.

The kingdom is at hand.
Still.
Always.

Grab it.
Train in it.
Live it out loud in the quiet places.

And one day, when my voice is just ink on a page, know this:

I'm still walking the road ahead, waiting at the next bend, cheering you on.

I love you.
More than words.

Now go start the revolution.

Unhurried. Unstoppable.

— Dad / Granddad

REFLECTION PROMPTS AND DISCUSSION QUESTIONS

To make this book a starting point for transformation, I've included 3–5 prompts per chapter. Use them solo for journaling, or in a group/family setting for deeper conversation. They're designed to bridge theory to practice—reflect, apply, and share. Tie back to Scripture where noted for a "deep dive" like in my previous books.

Chapter 1: The Offer Still Stands

What "eternal life" misconceptions did you grow up with? How does Jesus' invitation to "follow Me" change that?

Describe a moment when you've glimpsed the life Jesus describes (e.g., unshakable peace). What blocked it from becoming your default?

This week, identify one area (e.g., anxiety) where you'll say "yes" to His offer. What small step starts it?

Discuss: John 17:3—"This is eternal life: that they know you." How does "knowing" God differ from just believing facts?

Group: Share one barrier to following Jesus fully. Pray for breakthroughs.

Chapter 2: Jesus Dropped a Mic, Not a Religion

Count how many times "kingdom" appears in your Bible app (as suggested). What surprises you?

How has "religion" (rules, attendance) fallen short in your experience? Contrast with Jesus' kingdom announcement.

Reflect: Where have you seen "kingdom stuff" (healing, peace in chaos) in real life? If rarely, why?

Deep dive: Matthew 4:17—Jesus' first message. How would your week change if you lived like the kingdom is "at hand"?

Group: Brainstorm ways to "grab the kingdom" together this month.

Chapter 3: Consumer Christianity Is Bankrupt

List "transactions" you've made with God (e.g., attendance for blessings). How did they fail?

What "product" version of faith have you bought into? How does it keep you weak?

Reflect: "Lose your life to find it" (Matthew 16:25). What would "giving your whole life" look like practically?

Discuss: Signs of spiritual bankruptcy in your circle (e.g., exhaustion despite commitment).

Action: Replace one "consumer" habit (e.g., passive scrolling) with a "follower" practice this week.

Chapter 4: Apprentice, Not Fan

Are you more "fan" or "apprentice" right now? Give evidence from your daily responses (e.g., traffic temper).

What would "move in close and copy the Master" mean for your routines?

Reflect on a time "fandom" let you down. How could apprenticeship rewrite it?

Deep dive: Matthew 4:19—"Follow Me, and I will make you..." What is Jesus "making" you into?

Group: Commit to one apprenticeship experiment (e .g., patience training) and report back.

Chapter 5: The Curriculum of Christ

Which part of the Sermon on the Mount feels most "impossible"? Reframe it as a "target" you're training toward.

How have you viewed the Sermon—as guilt trip or invitation? Shift your perspective.

Journal: "Who am I becoming?" Tie to one Sermon trait (e.g., free from anxiety).

Discuss: Matthew 5-7 as "syllabus." What's your first "practice session"?

Action: Read the Sermon aloud this week; note one piece to "drive" with Jesus.

Chapter 6: Blessed Are the Broke

Which Beatitude doorway are you standing in right now (e.g., mourning, hungering)? How is it an invitation?

Reflect: A time brokenness led to blessing. If not, pray for eyes to see it.

How does "blessed are the broke" challenge success culture?

Deep dive: Matthew 5:3-12. Pick one and apply to a current struggle.

Group: Share a "broke" story anonymously; pray blessings over each.

Chapter 7: Your Secret Life Is the Real One

Inventory: What's in your "secret life" (e.g., hidden anger)? Invite Jesus in—journal the conversation.

How has "overflow" shown up lately (words/actions revealing heart)?

Reflect: One area (e.g., worry) to renovate this week.

Discuss: Matthew 6:21—"Where your treasure is, there your heart will be." Audit yours.

Action: Practice one "secret act" (e.g., private prayer) and note the reward.

Chapter 8: Stop Trying Harder (Start Training)

Recall a "try harder" failure. How would "training" change it?

Pick a target area; outline indirect efforts (e.g., gratitude for anxiety).

Reflect: "Grace opposes earning, not effort." How does this free you?

Deep dive: 2 Timothy 2:1–7—athlete/soldier/farmer metaphors for training.

Group: Share training plans; encourage weekly.

Chapter 9: Spiritual Disciplines Without the Religious Weirdness

Which discipline feels least "weird"? Try it this week—report shifts.

How could one (e.g., silence) combat your biggest distraction?

Reflect: A time a discipline (intentional or not) brought freedom.

Discuss: Pick from the five; adapt for your life stage.

Action: Experiment with one; adjust for "normal people" fit.

Chapter 10: Living the Kingdom in a Burnout Culture

Identify your top trap (e.g., social media). Apply a kingdom upgrade.

How has burnout culture stolen from you? Reclaim with one practice.

Reflect: A cultural "arrangement" to realign this month.

Deep dive: Matthew 6:24–34—money/worry as examples.

Group: Share traps anonymously; brainstorm counters.

Chapter 11: The Church as Training Camp, Not Museum

What's "cringe" about church for you? Reframe as training opportunity.

Reflect: A time community accelerated growth (or lack hindered it).

How can you "coach" your church toward camp mode?

Discuss: Acts 2:42–47—early church as model.

Action: Join/start a small training group.

Chapter 12: The Unhurried Revolution

What's one "mustard seed" act you'll start today?

Reflect: How does "unhurried" challenge your pace?

Envision: Your life/family in 5 years, kingdom-shaped.

Deep dive: Matthew 13:31–32—mustard seed parable.

Group: Commit to one revolutionary friendship or act.

Recommended Reading

These books shaped this one—start with Willard for depth, then branch out. I've annotated briefly to guide you. Focus on 1–2 at a time; they're dense but life-changing.

The Divine Conspiracy – Dallas Willard (1998)

Renovation of the Heart – Dallas Willard (2002)

The Spirit of the Disciplines – Dallas Willard (1988)

Hearing God – Dallas Willard (1984)

Practicing the Way – John Mark Comer (2024)

The Ruthless Elimination of Hurry – John Mark Comer (2019)

Celebration of Discipline – Richard Foster (1978)

The Sermon on the Mount and Human Flourishing – Jonathan Pennington (2017)

The Bible (ESV or NIV recommended)
Start with the Gospels and search "kingdom" every time it shows up.

GRACE ON A TUESDAY

Most of life won't be lived on Sundays.

It'll be lived on Tuesdays—when the alarm hits too early, when the calendar is rude, when the group chat is loud, when your mind is already sprinting before your feet touch the floor. Nothing dramatic. Just ordinary pressure. The kind that slowly turns sincere Christians into exhausted ones.

Here's what I mean.

When the kingdom stays theoretical, Tuesday becomes a treadmill. You wake up behind. You scroll before you pray. You carry yesterday's irritation like a backpack you never take off. You snap at people you love. You numb out with noise. You promise yourself you'll do better tomorrow—and then tomorrow turns into another Tuesday.

Grace still forgives you in that life.

But it doesn't feel like freedom.

It feels like survival.

And that is exactly what I don't want for you.

Because Jesus didn't just come to cover your sin. He came to give you His life—steady peace in real stress, real power in real temptation, real love in real relationships. Not when you finally get your act together. Not when the season calms down. Right in the middle of Tuesday.

That's the difference the gospel of the kingdom makes: it doesn't wait for perfect circumstances. It changes the air you breathe inside imperfect ones.

So before you close this book and step back into your week, let me give you one simple way to practice the kingdom on purpose—tomorrow.

The Tuesday Drill (10 minutes)

1 minute — Stop.
Feet on the floor. Phone down. Breathe. Say, "Father, Your kingdom is here."

3 minutes — Name the One Thing.
What's the biggest pressure you're carrying into today—fear, anger, lust, hurry, resentment? Name it plainly.

3 minutes — Listen.
Silence. No fixing. No rehearsing conversations. Just presence.

2 minutes — Hand it over.
"Jesus, I give You this. Teach me how to live today with You."

1 minute — Choose one small act.
One kingdom move before noon: bless someone, tell the truth, apologize, refuse the scroll, take the slower lane, pray for the person you resent.

That's it.

Not heroic. Not weird. Just training.

Do that for a month and you won't just "believe" in the kingdom—you'll start living in it. Tuesday will still be Tuesday. The calendar won't magically behave. But you will be different inside it. And that's where everything changes.

The offer still stands.

"Follow Me."

About the Author

Christian A. Dickinson writes for people who are tired of a faith that stays theoretical. Influenced deeply by Dallas Willard, his work centers on the gospel of the kingdom—life with God available now.

Raised in a living-room church and shaped by years of leadership, teaching, and coaching, he is passionate about translating deep spiritual truth into plain language that actually works in everyday life. He wrote this book first for his children and grandchildren, and offers it outward to anyone hungry for more than surface-level religion.

Christian is the founder of Learning Engineered Publishing®. More at learningengineeredpublishing.com.